LIGHTNING BOLT BOOKS™

Are You Ready for Summer?

Sheila Anderson

Lerner Publications Company

Minneapolis

To Anousone
Chiaokhiao

Lerner Publications Company
A division of Lerner Publishing Group, Inc.
241 First Avenue North
Minneapolis, MN 55401 U.S.A.

Website address: www.lernerbooks.com

Library of Congress Cataloging-in-Publication Data

Anderson, Sheila.
    Are you ready for summer? / by Sheila M. Anderson.
        p.   cm. — (Lightning bolt books™ – Our four seasons)
    Includes index.
    ISBN 978–0–7613–4585–5 (lib. bdg. : alk. paper)
    1. Summer—Juvenile literature. I. Title.
  QB637.6.A53 2010
    508.2—dc22   2009016410

Manufactured in the United States of America
1 – BP – 12/15/09

Contents

Sights and Sounds of Summer

Crrack! Listen to the sounds of children playing baseball in the park.

Summer is here.

Warm sunshine and clear, blue skies invite people to play outdoors.

Kids playing games are a common sight on sunny summer days.

Kids fly by on their bicycles and call to their friends.

Summer Weather

The air is hot. Dogs pant as they lie under shady, leaf-covered trees.

Two furry dogs cool off on a bench in the shade.

Grass grows thick
and green beneath
the blazing
summer sun.

In some places, the summer air is dry. It makes me thirsty for a cool glass of lemonade.

Four girls sell lemonade on a hot summer day.

In other places, summer air is humid. The moisture in the air feels thick and dewy.

The weather in Saint Petersburg, Florida, is often warm and humid.

11

Staying Cool

It's time to wear shorts and T-shirts. Sandals help keep my feet cool and protected from the sizzling hot sidewalk.

I rub sunscreen on my arms and legs. It protects my skin from the sun's scorching rays.

Help your friends put on sunscreen. Be careful not to miss a spot!

A floppy hat and dark sunglasses shade my eyes from the bright sunshine.

It's important to protect your eyes from the sun. Too much sunshine can hurt them.

Splash! Swimming is one way to stay cool in the summer. Sunlight sparkles like diamonds on the water.

Inside, a fan blows a cool breeze to keep us comfortable.

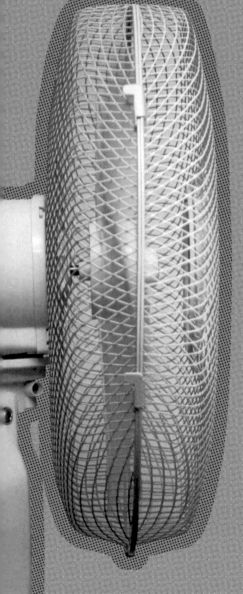

The Summer World

In summer, animals teach their young to hunt for food. Soon their babies will go off on their own.

A mother bear teaches her cubs how to catch fish.

Ducks swim with their babies
lined up close behind them.
Follow the leader!

Baby ducks are called ducklings.

Tree branches can barely be seen through puffs of deep green leaves.

Plants are covered with clusters of brightly colored flowers. Mmmmm. Smell their sweet scent.

Vegetables grow heavy on their vines. When they are ripe, we pick them. Maybe we'll make a salad.

Zucchini grow on vines in the summertime.

Some trees form acorns or other kinds of seeds.

Acorns grow on oak trees.

Days are long. The sun doesn't set until evening.

Fall Is Coming

In late summer, days begin to get shorter. The temperature begins to cool slightly.

In late summer, you might need a sweatshirt outside.

Leaves start to change color.

Children start thinking about going back to school.

What will you put in your backpack this year?

Fall is on its way.

Summer Solstice

The summer solstice happens each year around June 21. It marks the beginning of summer in the Northern Hemisphere.

The solstice occurs because Earth is tilted on an axis. An axis is an imaginary line through the middle of Earth. Earth moves around the sun on its axis. And since Earth is tilted, only one side leans toward the sun at a time. The side that is leaning toward the sun gets more sunlight than the side that is leaning away from it.

The Northern Hemisphere points most toward the sun around June 21. So that's why the solstice happens at this time.

Some cultures celebrate the summer solstice. People are thankful for the sunshine that helps plants grow. Plants produce food for people to eat. Fruits and vegetables will be ready to pick and eat soon after the summer solstice.

If you were to plan a summer solstice celebration, what would it be like?

In Sweden, people celebrate the summer solstice with dances and songs.

Glossary

cluster: a group of items such as flowers

humid: hot and sticky

moisture: dampness

protect: to keep safe

ripe: ready to be picked and eaten

scorching: very hot

sunscreen: a cream or lotion that protects skin from the sun

vine: a long, skinny branch

Further Reading

Branley, Franklyn M. *Sunshine Makes the Seasons.* New York: HarperCollins Publishers, 2005.

Enchanted Learning: Earth's Seasons http://www.enchantedlearning.com/subjects/astronomy/planets/earth/Seasons.shtml

Environmental Protection Agency: SunWise Kids http://www.epa.gov/SunWise/kids.html

Glaser, Linda. *It's Summer!* Minneapolis: Millbrook Press, 2003.

Low, Alice. *Summer.* New York: Random House, 2007.

Vanasse, Deb. *Under Alaska's Midnight Sun.* Seattle: Sasquatch Books, 2005.

Index

Photo Acknowledgments

The images in this book are used with the permission of: © Jonathan Vasata/
Dreamstime.com, p. 1; © Juana Van Burg/Dreamstime.com, p. 2; © BananaStock Ltd.,
p. 4; © Peter Muller/Cultura/Getty Images, p. 5; © Cheryl Casey/Dreamstime.com, p. 6;
© Lori Adamski Peek/The Image Bank/Getty Images, p. 7; © Egophoto/Dreamstime.
com, p. 8; © Asia Images Group/AsiaPix/Getty Images, p. 9; © Tony Anderson/Taxi/
Getty Images, p. 10; © Prisma/SuperStock, p. 11; © Saksoni/Dreamstime.com, p. 12;
© Odilon Dimier/PhotoAlto Agency RF Collections©Getty Images, p. 13; © Anne Flinn
Powell/Index Stock Imagery/Photolibrary, p. 14; © Oscar Mattsson/Nordic Photos/
Photolibrary, p. 15; © Nick Kennedy/Alamy, p. 16; © outdoorsman-Fotolia.com, p. 17;
© age fotostock/SuperStock, p. 18; © Boris Breuer/Digital Vision/Getty Images, p. 19;
© Michael Iwasaki/Dreamstime.com, p. 20; © Ilka-erika Szasz-fabian/Dreamstime.
com, p. 21; © istera-Fotolia.com, p. 22; © Jan Greune/LOOK/Getty Images, p. 23;
© Darrin Klimek/Taxi/Getty Images, p. 24; © Roswitha S. -Fotolia.com, p. 25; © Colin
Gray/Photonica/Getty Images, p. 26; © Peter Widmann/Alamy, p. 27; © Christophe
Testi/Dreamstime.com, p. 28; © Per Magnus Persson/Johner Images/Getty Images, p. 29;
© Barbara Peacock/Taxi/Getty Images, p. 30; © Timhope/Dreamstime.com, p.31.

Cover: © Photodisc/Getty Images.